OEDIPUS

Borgo Press Books by VOLTAIRE

The Death of Caesar: A Play in Three Acts
Oedipus: A Play in Five Acts
Saul and David: A Play in Five Acts
Socrates: A Play in Three Acts

OEDIPUS

A PLAY IN FIVE ACTS

VOLTAIRE

Translated and Adapted by Frank J. Morlock

THE BORGO PRESS
MMXII

OEDIPUS

Copyright © 2003, 2012 by Frank J. Morlock

FIRST BORGO PRESS EDITION

Published by Wildside Press LLC

www.wildsidebooks.com

DEDICATION

For My Friends,

Ron Landers and Jane Eaton

CONTENTS

CAST OF CHARACTERS 9
ACT I 11
ACT II 35
ACT III 63
ACT IV 91
ACT V 119
ABOUT THE AUTHOR 147

CAST OF CHARACTERS

OEDIPUS, King of Thebes

JOCASTA, Queen of Thebes

PHILOCTETES, Prince of Euboea

THE HIGH PRIEST

ARASPAS, confidant of Oedipus

AEGINA, confident of Jocasta

DIMAS, friend of Philoctetes

PHORBAS, old Theban

ICARUS, old Corinthian

CHORUS OF THEBANS

ACT I

DIMAS

Philoctetes, is it you? What frightful blow of fate

Makes you seek death in these infested climes?

Are you coming to affront the rage of our gods?

No mortal dares set a bold foot here.

These climes are filled with celestial wrath:

And devouring death dwells amongst us.

Thebes, long dedicated to horrors,

Seems to remain separated from the rest of the living.

Go back—

PHILOCTETES

This abode suits misfortunes:

Go: let me care for my frightful destiny

And tell me if the gods' inhuman wrath,

In overwhelming these people, has respected the Queen.

DIMAS

Yes, lord, she's living: but the contagion

Brings its poison to the foot of her throne.

Each moment steals a faithful servant from her.

And death, by degrees, seems to approach her.

They say that heaven, finally, after so much wrath

Is going to withdraw its heavy hand from us.

So much blood, so many deaths, ought to have satisfied it.

PHILOCTETES

Eh! What crime has produced a wrath so harsh?

DIMAS

Since the death of the king—

PHILOCTETES

What am I hearing? What! Laius?

DIMAS

Lord, for the last four years this hero has no longer been living.

PHILOCTETES

No longer living! What word has struck my ear!

What seducing hope in my heart is awakening!

What! Jocasta— The gods are being kinder to me?

What! Philoctetes at last can be yours?

He's no longer living!— What fate ended his life?

DIMAS

Four years have flowed by since, in Boeotia,

Fate guided your steps here for the last time.

Hardly had you left the breast of your estates,

Hardly had you taken the road to Asia,

When, by a perfidious blow, an enemy hand

Ravished this unfortunate prince from his subjects.

PHILOCTETES

What! Dimas, your master died assassinated?

DIMAS

That was the first beginning of our misfortune.

That crime dragged the empire to ruin.

The uproar of the mortal blows struck his death.

We were occupied shedding tears,

When, by the wrath of the god's shocking minister,

Fatal to the innocent without punishing the guilty,

A monster— (far away from us what were you doing then?)

A furious monster came to ravage these shores.

Heaven, industrious in its sad vengeance,

Had exhausted its power in forming it.

Born among rocks, at the foot of Citheron,

This monster with a human voice, agile, feminine and leonine,

An execrable assembly of all nature,

United against us, cunning with rage.

There was only one way to preserve these regions from it.

With a twisted sense insidious words,

The monster, each day, in terrified Thebes,

Pursued the feeble remainder escaped from death.

And if some mortal wanted to help us,

He had to see the monster and listen to it or perish.

To this terrible decree it was necessary to submit.

With a common voice Thebes offered its empire

To the happy interpreter inspired by the gods

Who would reveal to us the mysterious meaning.

Our sages, our wise men, seduced by hope,

Dared, on the faith of a vain science,

To confront the wrath of the impenetrable monster.

None of them understood it; they all expired.

But Oedipus, heir to the scepter of Corinth,

Young, in that happy age which doesn't know fear,

Led by fortune into these terrified parts,

Came, saw the monster, understood it, and was king.

He lives, he's still reigning, but his sad power

Sees only death under his obedience.

Alas! we flattered ourselves that his lucky hands

Enchained destiny forever to his throne.

Already, even the gods seemed more clever to us.

The monster expiring, left these walls in peace.

But sterility on this funereal shore

Soon, with famine, brought us death.

The gods have led us from torture to torture.

The famine has ceased, but not their injustice.

And the contagion, depopulating our estates,

Pursues a weak remnant that escaped death.

Such is the horrible condition to which the gods have reduced us.

But you, happy warrior that the gods favor,

What has been able to snatch you from the breast of glory?

What are you coming to seek in this frightful abode?

PHILOCTETES

I am coming here to bring my tears and my profound sorrow.

Know my misfortune and the misfortune of the world.

My eyes will no longer see this worthy son of gods.

This support of the world, invincible like them,

The oppressed innocent is losing his tutelary god.

I am weeping for my friend, the world is weeping for a father.

DIMAS

Hercules is dead?

PHILOCTETES

Friend, these unlucky hands

Have placed on the funeral pyre the greatest of humans.

I bring to these abodes his invincible arrows,

Dear and terrible presents of the son of Jupiter.

I bring his ashes, and come with this hero

Expecting altars raised to his tomb.

Trust me, if he had lived, if with such a rare present,

Heaven were to have been less avaricious for mortals,

I would have fulfilled my destiny far from Jocasta:

And with my passion reborn in my heart

You wouldn't see me following love for a guide

—Abandon Alcidas to serve a woman!

DIMAS

For a long while I've pitied this sweet and powerful passion.

It was born in childhood and grew up with you;

Jocasta, forced to her marriage by her father,

Was placed with regret on the throne of Laius.

Alas, by this marriage which cost so many tears,

The Fates were secretly preparing our misfortunes.

How I admire this supreme virtue in you,

This heart worthy of a throne and master of itself!

In vain love spoke to this agitated heart.

It was the first tyrant that you subdued.

PHILOCTETES

It was necessary to flee to conquer; yes, I confess it.

I struggled for some time; I sensed my weakness.

It was necessary to tear myself from this funereal place

And I bid Jocasta an eternal farewell.

Meanwhile, the universe, trembling at the name of Alcidas,

Awaited his destiny with its rapid valor;

I dared to associate myself with his divine works,

I marched with him, circled by the same laurels.

It's then indeed that my soul was enlightened;

Against the passions it felt itself assured.

The friendship of a great man is a blessing of the gods.

I read my duty and my fate in his eyes.

I apprenticed my virtues with him;

Without hardening my heart, I strengthened my courage,

Inflexible virtue enchained under its sway.

What would I have been without him? Nothing but the son of a king?

Nothing but a vulgar prince, and perhaps I would have been

Slave of my senses which he made me master of.

DIMAS

So then, henceforth, without pity and without wrath,

You will see Jocasta and her new spouse again?

PHILOCTETES

What do you mean! What are you saying? A new

marriage?

DIMAS

Oedipus has joined his fate to this queen.

PHILOCTETES

Oedipus is very lucky! I am not surprised by it;

And he who saved his people is worthy of such a reward.

Heaven is just.

DIMAS

Oedipus is going to appear in these parts.

All the people with him, led by the high priest,

Coming to conjure the harshness of the irritated gods.

PHILOCTETES

I feel myself softened, I share their tears.

O you, in the high heavens, watch over your country;

Hearken in its favor to a friend who prays to you:

Hercules, be the god of your fellow citizens.

Let their prayers rise to you with mine!

(Philoctetes leaves. The door of the temple opens and the High Priest appears in the midst of the people.)

FIRST CHARACTER IN THE CHORUS

Infectious spirits, tyrants of this empire

Who blow death in the air one breathes within these walls,

Increase against us your slow fury

And of too prolonged a death, spare us the horror.

SECOND CHARACTER

Strike, all powerful gods; your victims are prepared.

O mountains, crush us. Heavens, fall on our heads.

O death we implore your funereal aid.

O death, come save us, come end our lives.

HIGH PRIEST

Cease, and control your lamentations,

Weak solace to the ills of wretches.

Let's bend under a god who wishes to test us,

Who, with a word, can ruin us, and with a word, can save us.

He knows that in these walls death surrounds us

And the cries of Thebans have mounted to his throne.

The king is coming. Through my voice heaven is going to speak to him.

Fate to his eyes will be unveiled.

The time has arrived, this great day

The king and the people are going to change their fate.

(Enter Oedipus, Jocasta, Aegina, Araspas.)

OEDIPUS

People, who bring their sorrows into this temple,

Present to our gods offerings of tears.

Why cannot I divert their vengeance to myself,

Death which follows you chokes the germinating seed!

But, in this common danger, a king is only a man

And all that he can do is share it.

(to the High Priest)

You, minister of the gods adored in Thebes,

Are they still disdaining the voice that implores them?

Will they view without pity the end of our sad lives?

Are these masters of mortals mute and deaf?

THE HIGH PRIEST

King, people, hear me. Tonight, in my sight,

The flame of heaven descended to our altars.

The shade of the great Laius appeared among us,

Terrifying, and breathing hate and wrath.

Then a frightening voice made itself heard:

"The Thebans of Laius have not avenged his ashes.

The murderer of the king breathes in this community

And his impure breath infects our climate.

He must be known, he must be punished.

People, your safety depends upon his death."

OEDIPUS

Thebans, I will admit it, you are justly suffering

A rough punishment for an inexcusable crime.

Laius was dear to you and your neglect

Of his sacred Manes has betrayed vengeance.

Such is often the fate of the most just kings!

While they are on earth their laws are respected.

They take their supreme justice with them to heaven;

Adored by their people, they are gods themselves;

But after their death, what are they in your eyes?

You extinguish the ashes you were burning for them.

And as to self interest the human soul is bound,

Virtue that is no longer is soon forgotten.

Thus from heaven, imploring the wrath of an avenger

The blood of a king rises against you.

Let's appease his murmurs, and instead of a hecatomb

Let the blood of a murderer be poured over his tomb.

Let's apply all our efforts to find the guilty one.

What! to the death of a king there are no witnesses?

And you've been unable, amidst so many prodigies,

To find vestiges of this unpunished crime?

They've always told me that it was a Theban

Who raised a guilty hand to his prince.

(to Jocasta)

As for me, who, through your hands receiving his crown,

Mounted the throne two years after his death,

Madame, up to now, respecting your sorrows,

I have not recalled the subject of your tears:

And, by your own perils alarmed each day

My soul to other cares seemed to be shut.

JOCASTA

Lord, when destiny reserved me to you

By an unforeseen blow which took me from my spouse,

When, traveling through the frontiers of his kingdom,

This hero succumbed under murderous hands.

Phorbas in this trip was alone with him.

Phorbas was the councilor and support of the king.

Laius knew his zeal and his prudence,

Shared with him the weight of his power.

It was before his eyes that the prince was massacred.

He brought into our walls the disfigured corpse:

Pierced by blows himself, he could hardly drag himself.

He fell all bloody at the knees of his queen.

He said "Strangers have brought these great blows.

Before my eyes they massacred your spouse.

They left me dying; and the celestial power

Revived the remainder of my unhappy days."

He told me nothing more and my agitated heart

Saw the sad truth fleeing far from it.

And perhaps, heaven, irritated by this great crime,

Hid the guilty from my just pursuit.

Perhaps, accomplishing its eternal decrees

So as to punish us, it made us criminals.

Soon after the sphinx desolated this shore.

Thebes was attentive to its furors,

And in such terror was still unable

To avenge the death of another while trembling for oneself.

OEDIPUS

Madame, what became of this faithful subject?

JOCASTA

Lord, they paid his zeal and service ill.

In secret the whole realm was his enemy:

He was too powerful not to be hated.

And the people and the notables, in senseless wrath,

Were burning to punish his past favor.

They accused him of it, and by a common distraction

The whole of Thebes with great shouts demanded his death of me.

And as for me, suspecting injustice on all sides,

I trembled to order his pardon or his death.

Into a neighboring castle, escorted secretly,

I concealed his head from their distraction.

There, for four winters this venerable old geezer,

A deplorable example of the favor of kings,

Without complaining of me or the irritated populace

In his solitary innocence, awaits his liberty.

OEDIPUS (to his suite)

Madame, that's enough. Run, let them hurry

To open his prison, let him come, let him appear.

Before you, I myself intend to interrogate him.

I have all my people together and Laius to avenge.

We must hear all, we must strictly observe

And sound the depths of this sad mystery.

And you gods of Thebans, gods who exhaust us,

Punish the assassin, you who know him!

Sun, hide from his eyes the day that lights us!

Let him be a horror to his sons, execrable to his mother,

Wandering, abandoned, proscribed by the universe.

He gathers on himself all the ills of hell:

And may his bloody body, deprived of a sepulcher

Become the pasture of devouring vultures!

HIGH PRIEST

To these terrifying oaths we all join.

OEDIPUS

Gods, let the crime alone at last experience your blows!

Or, by your decrees of eternal justice

Abandon to my arm the care of his death

And if you are tired of hating us,

Give, by commanding, the power to obey.

If, on an unknown you are pursuing crime,

Finish your work and name the victim.

You, return to the temple; go, let your voice

Question the gods a second time.

Let your prayers force them to descend amongst us.

If they loved Laius they will avenge his ashes.

And, leading a king easily deceived,

They will point out the place where my arm ought to strike.

CURTAIN

ACT II

ARASPAS

Yes, this expiring people, whose interpreter I am,

With a common voice accuse Philoctetes,

Madame, and the fates in this sad abode,

To save us, doubtless, have permitted his return.

JOCASTA

Great gods, what have I heard!

AEGINA

My surprise is extreme!

JOCASTA

Who? Him! Who? Philoctetes!

ARASPAS

Yes, Madame, himself.

To who else, indeed, could they impute

A murder that before our eyes he seemed to meditate?

He hated Laius, they know it; and his hate

Was hardly hidden before the eyes of your spouse.

Imprudent youth easily betrayed itself.

His ill disguised face revealed his scorn.

I'm unaware what subject animated his rage

But to the single name of king, too prompt and too sincere

Slave of a wrath he could not subdue,

Even to threats he dared be carried away.

He left, and since then, his errant destiny

Brought to our shores his floating fortune.

Even he was in Thebes in those unhappy times

That heaven marked by a frightful parricide.

Since that fatal day, with some probability,

Our people have distrusted him.

What do I say? The suspicions of Thebans for a long enough while

Floated uncertainly between him and Phorbas.

Still that great name that he received in war,

That famous title of avenger of the earth,

That respect we bear to heroes despite ourselves,

Made us silence our suspicions, and suspend our blows.

But the times are changed: Thebes on this funereal day

Of a dangerous respect strips off the rest.

Vainly his glory speaks to these agitated hearts.

The gods want his blood and are alone heard.

FIRST CHARACTER OF THE CHORUS

O queen! have pity on a people who love you;

Mitigate the supreme justice of these gods;

Deliver to us their victim; address our prayers to them

Who can better touch them than a heart so worthy of them?

JOCASTA

To soften their wrath, if it merely required my life,

Alas! It's without regret that I would sacrifice it.

Thebans who still believe some virtues in me,

I offer you my blood: don't exact anything more.

Go!

(Araspas and the Chorus leave.)

AEGINA

How I pity you!

JOCASTA

Alas! I envy

Those who in these walls ended their life.

What a situation! What torture for a virtuous heart.

AEGINA

There's no further doubt, your fate is frightful!

These people, that are blindly driven by a false zeal,

Will soon, with great shouts, demand their victim.

I don't dare accuse him; but what horror for you

If, in him, you find the murderer of a spouse!

JOCASTA

And to dare to do such an outrage to the two of them!

Crime and baseness would have been his share!

Aegina, after the bonds that he failed to break,

All I lack to my ills is to hear him accused.

Know that these suspicions irritate my wrath

And that he is virtuous since he knew how to please me.

AEGINA

That love, so constant—

JOCASTA

Don't believe that my heart

Was able to nourish the passion of that funereal love.

I fought it too much. Still, dear Aegina,

Do what it can, a great heart dominated by virtue,

Cannot hide these secret movements

Of indomitable children of nature in us.

In the folds of the soul they come to surprise us

These fires that one believes extinguished

Are reborn from their ashes.

And strict virtue, in these harsh struggles,

Resists passions and doesn't destroy them.

AEGINA

Your sorrow is just, as well as virtuous,

And with such feelings.

JOCASTA

How wretched I am!

Dear Aegina, you know, both my heart and my ills.

I've twice lit the marriage torch,

Twice submitted to the injustice of my fate.

I've changed slavery, or rather torment,

And the only mortal by whom my heart was touched

Must be forever torn from my prayers

Pardon me, great gods, this funeral souvenir

Of a flame I've mastered, it's the unhappy reminder.

Aegina, you saw us charmed by one another.

You saw the bonds broken as soon as they formed.

My sovereign loved me, obtained me despite myself.

My face, weighed with troubles was circled with a diadem.

We must forget, in his kisses,

My first love and my first oaths.

You know that, completely attached to my duty,

I suffocated the rebellion of my hidden feelings,

That, disguising my confusion and devouring my tears,

I didn't dare confess my sorrows to myself.

AEGINA

How could you tempt destiny

With the yoke of matrimony a second time?

JOCASTA

Alas!

AEGINA

Is it permitted to hide nothing from you?

JOCASTA

Speak.

AEGINA

Oedipus appears to touch you, madame,

And your heart, at least without too much resistance,

Rewarded him for saving your estates.

JOCASTA

Ah! Great gods!

AEGINA

Was he luckier than Laius,

Or absent Philoctetes no longer touched you?

Between these two heroes were you shared?

JOCASTA

By a cruel monster Thebes was then ravaged.

My faith was promised to his liberator

And the conqueror of the Sphinx was worthy of me.

AEGINA

You loved him?

JOCASTA

I felt some tenderness for him.

But that feeling came from weakness!

Aegina, it wasn't a tumultuous fire

Of my enchanted senses of an impetuous child.

I didn't recognize this burning flame

That only Philoctetes was able to give birth to in my soul,

And which spread poison throughout my spirit,

With its fatal charm had seduced my reason.

I felt for Oedipus a grave friendship.

Oedipus is virtuous, his virtue was dear to me.

My heart saw him raised to the throne

Of the Thebans he had saved with pleasure.

Still, dragged to the altar on his heels,

Aegina, I felt in my astonished soul

Unknown distractions that I hadn't conceived.

Finally, with horror, I saw myself in his arms.

This marriage was concluded under a frightful omen,

Aegina, I saw in one dark night

Hell, near Oedipus and myself

Eternal abysses opening beneath my feet,

The shade of my first spouse, pale and bloody

Appeared frightful and threatening in this abyss.

He showed me my son, that son who in my flank

Had been formed from his unfortunate blood,

That son which my pious and barbarous injustice

Had made a secret sacrifice to our gods.

They seemed to order me to follow both of them.

The two of them seemed to drag me to Tartarus.

Confused feeling possessed my soul,

Always presenting this terrible idea.

And Philoctetes, still very present in my heart,

Increased the terror of this fatal confusion.

AEGINA

I hear some noise, they're coming, I see him coming forward.

JOCASTA

It's himself: I am trembling; let's avoid his presence.

(Aegina leaves, Philoctetes enters.)

PHILOCTETES

Don't flee, madam, and stop trembling.

Dare to see me, dare to hear me and speak to me.

Don't fear any more that my jealous tears

Will trouble the new charms of your happy marriage.

Don't expect shameful; reproaches from me

Nor cowardly sighs unworthy of both of us.

I won't trouble you with these vulgar speeches

That suggest delight to ordinary lovers.

A heart that cherishes you, and if more must be said

A heart for which yours had some tenderness

Hasn't learned to show you weakness.

JOCASTA

Such sentiments aren't yours alone.

I ought to give the example of them, or take it from you.

If Jocasta didn't know how to be united with you

It is right, above all, that she justify herself.

Lord, I loved you: a supreme law

Has always, despite myself, disposed of me.

Both from the Sphinx and gods the fury is very well known.

You know what the plagues have burst over us

And that Oedipus—

PHILOCTETES

I know that Oedipus is your spouse.

I know that he is worthy to be so, and despite his youth

The empire of Thebes was saved by his wisdom,

His exploits, his virtues, and especially, your choice

Put this lucky prince in the rank of the greatest kings.

Ah! Why has fortune, constantly injurious to me,

Brought otherwise to my imprudent valor?

If the conqueror of the Sphinx ought to conquer you

Did you have to search far away to perish?

I would not have pierced the frivolous gloom

With a vain meaning disguised under obscure words;

This arm that is still animated by your look

Would have brought the head of the monster to your knees.

Jocasta is still the conquest of another;

Another has been able to enjoy this excess of honor!

JOCASTA

You don't know what your misfortune is.

PHILOCTETES

I lost Alcidas and you; what is there left for me to fear?

JOCASTA

You are in abodes that a vengeful god abhors.

A deathly contagion announces his wrath

And the blood of Laius has fallen back on us.

From heaven, which pursues us with outraged justice,

This king's neglected ashes also seek vengeance.

We must on our altars sacrifice the assassin.

They seek him, they name you, they accuse you at last.

PHILOCTETES

Madam, I am silent, such an offense

Astonishes my courage and forces me to silence.

Who? Me, such felonies! Me, murder!

And that your spouse— You don't believe it.

JOCASTA

No, I don't believe it and it's an injury to you

To deign to combat imposture.

Your heart is known to me, you've had my faith

And you cannot be unworthy of me.

Forget these Thebans that the gods are abandoning,

Very worthy of perishing since they suspect you.

Flee me, it's over: we loved in vain,

The gods are reserving for you a most noble destiny;

You are born for them: their profound wisdom

Cannot settle in Thebes an arm useful to the world.

Don't allow love, filling that great heart,

To enchain near me your obscure valor.

No, with a charming bond, the tender and timid care

Must not occupy the successor of Alcidas.

Of all your virtues pertaining to their needs,

It's only to the unfortunate that you owe your efforts.

Tyrants are already reappearing on all sides.

Hercules is in the tomb and monsters are reborn:

Go, free from passions with which you were in love;

Leave, return Hercules to a startled universe.

Lord, my husband's coming; allow me to leave you.

Not that my troubled heart suspects its weakness,

But I would have too much to blush for before you

Since I loved you and he is my husband.

(Jocasta leaves. Enter Oedipus and Araspas.)

OEDIPUS

So that's the prince, Philoctetes there, Araspas?

PHILOCTETES

Yes, the one that blind fate in these walls

To his animated ruin, and that heaven once again,

Has made to suffer unaccustomed assaults.

I know what felonies they intend to darken my life with.

Lord, don't expect me to justify myself;

I have too much esteem for you and I don't think

That you could descend to such low suspicions.

If we are marching on the same path

My glory is closely enough associated with yours.

Theseus, Hercules, and I, we have demonstrated

The path to glory that you have taken.

Don't dishonor it by a slander on

The splendor of these names with which yours is allied.

And especially support, by a generous act,

The honor that you have been placed near them.

OEDIPUS

To be useful to mankind and to save this empire,

That, Lord, that is the only honor to which I aspire,

And in these extremities what I've been taught,

The heroes that I admire and that you imitate.

Surely, I don't wish to impute a crime to you.

If heaven had left me the choice of the victim,

I would not have sacrificed any other victim than myself.

To die for his country is the duty of a king.

It's an honor too great to cede to others.

I would have given my life and defended yours.

I would have saved my people a second time.

But, Lord, I haven't the liberty of choice,

It's a criminal blood that we must shed.

You are accused, think of defending yourself.

Appear innocent, it will be very pleasant for me

To honor in my court a hero such as you.

And I find myself happy, if I must treat you,

Not like an accused, but like Philoctetes.

PHILOCTETES

I must really admit it, on the faith of my name

I really dared to think myself above suspicion.

In default of thunder, this hand they accuse

Has delivered the earth from infamous assassins.

Hercules subdued them instructed by my arm.

Lord, he who punishes them does not imitate them.

OEDIPUS

Ah! I am not thinking of anything but exploits conse-
   crated

By your hands were dishonored by felonies.

Lord, and if Laius fell under your blows,

Doubtless with honor he expired under you;

You conquered him as a magnanimous warrior,

I am doing you too much justice.

PHILOCTETES

Eh! What would my crime be?

If Laius had been made to fall among the dead by this sword

It would have been for me only one triumph the more.

For his subjects a king is a god they revere;

For Hercules and me he's an ordinary man.

I've defended kings, and you must think

That I've been able to fight them, having been able to avenge them.

OEDIPUS

I know Philoctetes by these illustrious signs.

Warriors like you are the equals of monarchs.

I know it, still, prince, don't doubt it.

The conqueror of Laius is worthy of death;

His head will answer for the misfortunes of the empire

And you—

PHILOCTETES

It wasn't me; that word ought to suffice for you.

Lord, if it was me, I'd be vain about it.

In speaking to you thus, I ought to be listened to;

It's to common men, to ordinary souls,

To justify themselves in vulgar ways.

But a prince, a warrior, such as you, such as me,

When he says a thing, he's believed on his word.

Oedipus suspects me of the murder of Laius.

Ah! it isn't up to you to accuse anyone.

His scepter and his spouse have passed into your arms

It's you who are receiving the fruit of his death.

It's not I, who had the happy audacity

To dispute over his spoils and demand his place.

The throne is an object which could not tempt me.

Hercules disdained to climb to this high rank.

Ever free with him, without subjects and without master,

I've made sovereigns and I haven't wanted to be one.

But it's too much for me to defend myself and too humiliating.

Virtue is degraded by justifying itself.

OEDIPUS

Your virtue is dear to me, and your pride offends me.

You will be judged, prince, and if your innocence

Has nothing to fear from the equity of the law,

It must burst out with more splendor.

Stay amongst us.

PHILOCTETES

No question, I will remain.

It distracts from my glory and heaven which listens to me

Won't see me leave until avenged of the affront

By which your shameful suspicions have made my face blush.

(Exit Philoctetes.)

OEDIPUS

I will confess, I have trouble believing culpable

A heart of such unshakable audacity;

It doesn't know how to abase itself in disguises.

The liar doesn't have such high feelings;

I cannot see in him this base infamy.

I will tell you more: I was blushing in my soul

To see myself obliged to accuse this great heart.

I pity myself for my over harshness.

Cruel necessity attaches to empire.

Kings cannot read in human hearts.

Often they make blows fall on innocence,

And, Araspas, we are unjust despite ourselves.

But how slow Phorbas is for my impatience!

It's on him alone that I have some hope

For the irritated gods are no longer responding to us.

They have by their silence explained their refusal.

ARASPAS

While by your efforts you can learn all,

What need has heaven to make itself heard?

These gods whose pontiff has promised aid

Are no longer inhabiting their temples, Lord.

No one sees their arms so prodigal in miracles;

These caverns, these tripods which render their oracles

These bronzed oracles erected by our hands

Are not always animated by a pure breath.

We can no longer slumber trusting in priests;

Traitors are often at the foot of the sanctuary,

Who enslave us under a sacred power

Cause the facts to speak, and make them silent at their whim.

Look, examine with extreme care,

Philoctetes, Phorbas, and Jocasta herself.

Trust no one except ourselves: let's look everywhere under our eyes.

They are our tripods, our oracles, our gods.

OEDIPUS

Could there be in the temple such a perfidious heart?

No, it's still heaven that decides our fates.

It won't see placed in unworthy hands,

The precious treasury of the safety of Thebans.

I am going, I am going myself, to accuse their silence,

With my repeated prayers to soften their lack of clemency.

You, if to serve me you are showing some ardor,

Run to hasten the delay of Phorbas whom I'm awaiting.

In the deplorable condition in which you see us,

I intend to interrogate both gods and men.

CURTAIN

ACT III

JOCASTA

Yes, I'm awaiting Philoctetes, and I intend that for the last time

He appear before my eyes in these parts.

AEGINA

Madame, you know with what insolence

The license of the populace has made their shouting mount.

These Thebans besieged on all sides by death

Await their salvation only through his punishment.

Old geezers, women, children, overwhelmed by their misfortune,

All are interested in finding him guilty.

You can hear from here their seditious cries.

They demand his blood on behalf of the gods.

Can you resist so much violence?

Can you help him and take his defense?

JOCASTA

Me! Yes, I will take it! Were all the Thebans

To lay on me their parricidal hands,

Were I to be crushed under these smouldering walls,

I will not betray accused innocence.

But a just fear concerns my spirits;

My heart was once taken with this hero.

They know it; they will say that I am sacrificing to him

My glory, my spouse, my gods, and my country,

That my heart still burns.

AEGINA

Ah! Calm this terror.

This unfortunate love had no other witness than me:

And never—

JOCASTA

What are you saying? Do you think that a princess

Can ever hide her hate or her tenderness?

From every side the avid looks

Of courtiers fall on us.

Through respect their deceitful wiliness

Penetrates our hearts and seeks our weaknesses.

Nothing can escape or flee their malignity.

A single word, a sigh, a glance, betrays us.

Everything tells against us, even our silences.

And if their artifice and their perseverance

Finally, despite us, snatches away our secrets,

Their deceitful cunning bursts out,

Shedding a sad light on our life,

Filling the whole earth with our passions.

AEGINA

Eh! What's wrong with you, madam, to fear their blows?

What glances can be so piercing as to be dangerous to you?

What penetrated secret can wither your glory?

If they know your love, they know your victory.

They know that virtue has always been your support.

JOCASTA

And it's that virtue which troubles me today,

Always prompt and severe to accuse me.

I place on myself a glance too strict

And possibly judge myself too harshly.

But still, Philoctetes reigned in my heart,

In this unhappy heart where his image is traced,

Neither virtue nor time have been able to erase it.

What am I saying? I don't know, if I am saving his life,

If only justice is calling me to his aid.

My pity seems to me too tender and sensitive.

I feel my trembling arm very ready to defend him.

In the end I reproach myself for my shame and my efforts,

I would serve him better if I had loved him less.

AEGINA

But do you want him to leave?

JOCASTA

Yes, no question I want that.

It's my only hope and for the little he listens to me,

For the little my prayers have power over him,

He must prepare himself to never see me again.

Let him remove himself, let him flee these funereal abodes.

By distancing himself let him save his life and my glory.

But who can keep him? He ought to be here,

Dear Aegina, go, run.

(enter Philoctetes)

Ah! Prince, here you are!

In the mortal terror with which my soul is troubled,

I don't excuse myself from seeking your sight.

It's true, my duty directs me to flee you.

I must forget you and not betray you.

I think you know the fate they are preparing for you.

PHILOCTETES

A vain populace in tumult has demanded my head.

They are suffering, they are unjust, they must be pardoned.

JOCASTA

Beware of abandoning yourself to their furies.

Leave: you are still master of your fate.

But Lord, this moment is possibly the last

In which I can save you from an unworthy death.

Flee, and hurry your steps far from me.

As a reward for happily saving your life,

Forget that it was I who conserved it for you.

PHILOCTETES

Madam, deign to show to my agitated heart

Less compassion and greater firmness.

Prefer, as I do, honor to life.

Direct me to die and not to flee,

And don't force me, when I am innocent

To become guilty by obeying you.

Of the wealth that the celestial wrath has ravished me of,

My honor, my glory, alone remain to me.

Don't separate me from this wealth of which I am jealous.

I've lived, I've fulfilled my sad destiny.

My word has been given to your spouse, Madam.

Whatever unworthy suspicion he may have conceived of me,

I still don't know how to break my word.

JOCASTA

Lord, in the name of the gods, in the name of that passion

With which the sad Jocasta touched your soul,

If from such a perfect and tender friendship

You still retain some pity,

Finally, if you remember that, promised to each other

My happiness once depended on yours,

Deign to save your glory surrounded life,

A life that was fated to mine.

PHILOCTETES

I will consecrate it to you; I intend that its career

Be entirely worthy of you, of your virtues.

I've lived far from you, but my fate is very happy

If, dying, I bear your esteem to the tomb.

Who knows, even, who knows if with a propitious look

Heaven won't view this bloody sacrifice?

Who knows if its clemency, in the breast of your realm,

It hasn't led my steps here to sacrifice me?

Possibly it owes me this infinite mercy

Of preserving your life at the expense of mine?

Possibly it may be satisfied with pure blood,

And mine is worthy enough that it deigns to accept it.

(Enter Oedipus, Araspas and followers.)

OEDIPUS

Prince, have no fear of an impetuous caprice,

Of a populace whose voice demands your sacrifice.

I've calmed their tumult, if necessary,

I am coming to you to present my support.

They've suspected you; the populace had a duty to do so.

As for me, I don't judge like the rabble.

I intend that, piercing an odious cloud,

Your innocence shall burst out before their eyes.

My uncertain wit, which has been unable to decide anything,

Dares not condemn you, but is unable to absolve you.

So to heaven, I implore to decide me.

This heaven, at last appeased, intends to pardon us,

And soon, retracting the hand that has oppressed us

Through the voice of the high priest is naming the victim.

And I leave it to our gods, more enlightened than we

The duty of deciding between my people and you.

PHILOCTETES

Lord, your justice is inflexible and pure.

But extreme justice is an extreme injury.

You mustn't always listen to its harshness.

The first law we follow is honor.

I see myself reduced to the insult of responding

To vile detractors that I've known too well how to confound.

Ah! Without your abasing yourself to this unworthy duty,

Lord, it sufficed for me alone to be witness.

It was, it was enough to examine my life.

Hercules, supported by the gods, and conqueror of Asia,

Monsters, tyrants, that he taught me to subdue

These are the witnesses that must confront me,

Still question the mouthpiece of your gods.

We will learn from him if their voice condemns me.

I have no need of them and I await their decree,

From pity for this people and not from interest.

(Enter the High Priest and the Chorus.)

OEDIPUS

Well! The gods, touched by the prayers addressed to them,

Are they at last suspending their furious vengeance?

What parricidal hand has been able to offend them?

PHILOCTETES

Speak, whose is the blood we must shed?

THE HIGH PRIEST

Fatal gift of heaven! Unhappy science,

Dangerous to curious mortals,

Let it rain on the cruel fates revealed to me.

Would that an eternal veil covered my eyes.

PHILOCTETES

Well! What sinister thing have you come to announce?

OEDIPUS

Are you the minister of an eternal hate?

PHILOCTETES

Fear not.

OEDIPUS

Do the gods wish my death?

HIGH PRIEST (to Oedipus)

Ah! If you would trust me, don't question me.

OEDIPUS

Whatever may be the fate heaven is announcing to us,

The safety of Thebans depends on its response.

PHILOCTETES

Speak.

OEDIPUS

Have pity on so many unfortunates.

Believe that Oedipus—

HIGH PRIEST

Oedipus is more to be pitied than they.

FIRST CHARACTER IN THE CHORUS:

Oedipus has a paternal love for his people.

We join our eternal complaint to his voice

You to whom heaven speaks, hear our outcry.

SECOND CHARACTER OF THE CHORUS

We are dying, save us, deflect its furies,

Name this assassin, this monster, this liar.

FIRST CHARACTER OF THE CHORUS

Our arms are going to wash in the blood of his parricide.

HIGH PRIEST

Unfortunate people, what are you demanding of me?

FIRST CHARACTER IN THE CHORUS

Say one word, he dies and we are all saved.

HIGH PRIEST

When you are informed of the fate that is overwhelming him,

You will shiver in horror at the very name of the guilty.

The god who by my voice speaks to you at this moment

Commands that exile be his only punishment.

But soon, testing a funereal despair,

His hands will add to the celestial harshness.

Your eyes will be shocked by his terrible death

And you will believe your lives well paid for at this price.

OEDIPUS

Obey.

PHILOCTETES

Speak.

OEDIPUS

This is too much resistance.

THE HIGH PRIEST (to Oedipus)

It's you who are forcing me to break silence.

OEDIPUS

How these delays ignite my wrath.

HIGH PRIEST

You wish it— Well!— It's—

OEDIPUS

Get it over with, who?

HIGH PRIEST

You.

OEDIPUS

Me?

HIGH PRIEST

You, wretched prince!

SECOND CHARACTER OF THE CHORUS

Ah! What have I just heard?

JOCASTA

What are you daring to teach us, interpreter of gods?

(to Oedipus)

Who, you! You would be the assassin of my spouse?

You to whom I gave my crown and my hand?

No, lord, no: the oracle of the gods is abusing us.

Your virtue gives the lie to the voice that accuses you.

FIRST CHARACTER OF THE CHORUS

O heaven, whose power presides over our fate,

Name another head or render us dead.

PHILOCTETES

Lord, don't expect outrage for outrage.

I will not extract an unworthy advantage

Of the unheard of reversal that presses you before my eyes.

I believe you innocent despite the voice of the gods.

I am rendering you the justice that in the end is your due

And that this populace and you didn't render me.

Against your enemies, I offer you my arm,

Between a pontiff and you I do not hesitate.

A priest, whoever he may be, whatever the god that inspires him,

Must pray for his kings and not curse them.

OEDIPUS

What excess of virtue! But what summit of horror!

The one speaks like a demi-god, the other as an impostor priest.

(to the High Priest)

This is what the privilege of altars are!

To your sacrilegious mouth, mercy to impunity.

To accuse your king of an odious felony

Abuses insolently communication with the gods!

You think that my wrath must yet respect

The holy ministry that your hand dishonors.

Traitor, you must be sacrificed at the foot of the altars

In the presence of your gods that your voice makes speak.

HIGH PRIEST

My life is in your hands, you are the master of it.

Profit by the moments that you have to be so:

Today your sentence will be announced.

Tremble, wretched king, your reign is over.

An invisible hand suspends over your head

The threatening sword that vengeance is preparing.

Soon, you yourself, shocked by your felonies,

Fleeing far from this throne which you mounted,

Deprived of sacred fires and healthy water,

Filling with your screams solitary caves,

You will feel the blows of a vengeful god everywhere;

You will seek death; death will flee from you.

Heaven, this heaven, witness to so many funereal objects,

Will have no more for your eyes except horrible shadows.

To crime, to punishment, you are destined despite yourself.

You would be very lucky never to have been born.

OEDIPUS

To this point I've controlled my wrath to listen to you.

If your blood deserved that one deigned to shed it.

By your just death my satisfied glances,

Would forestall the effects of your prediction.

Go, flee, don't excite the distraction which agitates me

And respect a wrath which your presence irritates

Flee, abominable author of an unworthy lie.

HIGH PRIEST

You are still treating me as a traitor and impostor.

Your father used to think me more sincere.

OEDIPUS

Stop: what are you saying? Who? Polybius, my father—

HIGH PRIEST

You will very soon learn your funereal fate.

This day is going to give you birth and death.

Your fate is completed, you are going to know yourself.

Wretch! Do you know whose blood gave you being?

Surrounded by felonies reserved to you alone,

Do you even know with whom you are living?

O Corinth! O Phocidas! execrable marriage!

I see born an unlucky, impious race

Worthy of it's birth and by whom the furor

Will fill the universe with shock and horror.

We are leaving.

(Exit High Priest and his suite.)

OEDIPUS

These last words render me motionless.

I don't know where I am; my fury is calm.

It seems to me that a god descended amongst us,

Master of my distraction, enchaining my wrath

And loaning to a pontiff a divine force

Whose terrible voice announced my ruin to me.

PHILOCTETES

Lord, if you had to fear only kings,

Philoctetes would struggle with you under your rule.

But a priest here is more formidable,

Piercing you before our eyes with a respectable dart

Strongly supported by vain oracles.

A pontiff is often terrible to sovereigns

And, in its blind zeal, an opinionated populace,

Imbecilicly idolatrous of his sacred bonds,

Besmirching from piety the most holy laws,

Believes in honoring its gods by betraying its kings.

Especially, when interest, the father of license

Has just emboldened their impious zeal.

OEDIPUS

Ah! Lord, your virtues increase my sorrows,

The grandeur of your soul equals my misfortunes,

Overwhelmed by the weight of cares which are devouring me,

To try to comfort me is to overwhelm me further.

What plaintive voice is crying in the depth of my heart?

What crime have I committed? Is it true, vengeful god?

JOCASTA

Lord, that's enough, let's not speak any more of crime.

These expiring people must have a victim.

The state must be saved and it's much to delay it.

Wife of Laius, it's up to me to expire.

It's up to me to search for the infernal shore,

For the wandering and plaintive shade of an unfortunate spouse:

I will appease the screams of his bloody Manes;

I shall go— Let the gods be satisfied at this price,

Content with my death not to exact any other,

And that my blood poured out may be able to save yours!

OEDIPUS

You, die! You, madam! Ah! It's not enough

That so many frightful ills be amassed on my head?

Stop, queen, stop this terrible talk.

The fate of your husband is already too horrible

Without new darts coming to tear me apart,

You would give me yet your death to weep over?

Follow on my steps, let's go back in; I must enlighten myself

Over a suspicion I'm all too justly forming.

Come.

JOCASTA

What, lord, you could—

OEDIPUS

Follow me

And come dissipate or complete my terror.

CURTAIN

ACT IV

OEDIPUS

No, despite what you said, my uneasy soul

Is no less agitated by importunate suspicions.

The High Priest annoys me, and ready to excuse him

I begin, in secret, to accuse myself,

On all that he told me, full of supreme horror,

I am in secret interrogating myself.

And a thousand events effaced from my soul

Are offering themselves crowdedly to my frozen spirit.

The past forbids me, and the present overwhelms me

I read a shocking fate in the future

And crime everywhere seems to follow on my heels.

JOCASTA

Eh what! Your virtue doesn't reassure you!

Aren't you still sure of your innocence?

OEDIPUS

One can be more criminal than one knows.

JOCASTA

Ah! Disdaining the furors from an indiscreet priest,

Stop excusing him by these cowardly terrors.

OEDIPUS

In the name of great Laius and celestial wrath,

When Laius undertook this funeral voyage,

Did he have with him some guards, some soldiers?

JOCASTA

I already told you, only one followed his steps.

OEDIPUS

One lone man.

JOCASTA

This king, greater than his fortune,

Like you, disdained an importunate pomp.

No one was ever seen to walk before his chariot

With a numerous battalion's ostentatious guard.

In the midst of subjects submissive to his power

As if he was fearless, he walked without protection.

He thought himself protected by the love of his people.

OEDIPUS

O hero! Granted to mortals by heaven

Of true kings an august and rare example!

Has Oedipus on you laid his barbarous hand?

Depict for me at least this wretched prince.

JOCASTA

Since you recall an irritating memory

Despite the cold of his years, in his masculine age

His eyes still shone with the fire of his youth,

His scarred face under his white hair

Impressed respect on speechless mortals;

And Lord, if I dare to say what I am thinking

Laius had with you much resemblance

And I congratulated myself in re-finding in you

The virtues as well as the features of my spouse.

Lord, what is there in this speech that ought to shock you?

OEDIPUS

I espy misfortunes that I cannot comprehend.

I fear that the pontiff inspired by gods

Did not very much clarify my frightful destiny.

Me, could I have massacred! Gods, could it be possible?

JOCASTA

Is this organ of the gods infallible?

A holy ministry attaches them to altars.

They approach the gods, but they are mortals.

Do you really think, that at the whim of their request

The truth depends on the flight of their birds?

That under a sacred sword shivering bulls

Unveil the future to their piercing glances?

And that their victims decorated with festoons

Reveal human destiny in their flanks?

No, no: to seek for obscure truth this way

Is to usurp the rights of The Divinity.

Our priests are not what a vain people believe;

Our credulity is the foundation of all their science.

OEDIPUS

Ah, gods! If it's true, what would be my happiness!

JOCASTA

Lord, it's very true; believe in my sorrow.

Like you I was once preoccupied by them,

Alas! For my misfortune I was really self deceived.

And heaven punished me for having listened too much

To the false obscurity of an oracular imposter.

It cost me my son. Oracles that I abhor!

Without your order, but for you, my son would still be living.

OEDIPUS

Your son! By what blow did you lose him?

What oracle did the gods deliver to you?

JOCASTA

Learn, learn, in this extreme peril

What I wanted to hide even from myself.

And don't be further alarmed by a false oracle.

Lord, you know, I had a son by Laius.

My uneasy tenderness made me consult

Our gods' famous interpreter on the fate of my son.

What madness, alas! To want to snatch

Secrets that fate wished to hide from us!

But in the end I was a mother and full of weakness.

I cast my self fearfully at the feet of the priestess.

Here are her own words, I ought to have kept them.

Pardon, if I tremble at this sole memory.

"Your son will kill his father, and this sacrilegious son,

Incestuous and parricidal—" O gods! Shall I finish?

OEDIPUS

Well, madame?

JOCASTA

In the end, Lord, they predicted to me

That my son, that this monster, would enter into my bed.

That I would receive him, me, Lord, me, his mother,

Dripping in my arms from the murder of his father.

And that the two of us, joined by these frightful bonds,

I would give sons to my unfortunate son.

You are troubled lord, at this funereal tale.

You fear listening to me and to hear the rest.

OEDIPUS

Ah! Madam, finish: say what you did

With this child, the object of celestial wrath?

JOCASTA

I believed the gods, lord, and piously cruel

I suffocated my maternal love for my son.

In vain the imperious voice of that love

Opposed itself to our gods and condemned their laws.

It was necessary to hide this tender victim

From the fatal influence which was leading him to crime.

And thinking of triumphing over the horrors of his fate

From pity I ordered that they give him death.

O pity more criminal than wretched!

O by a falsely obscure deceitful oracle!

What fruit is returning to me from my barbarous efforts

My wretched spouse expired nonetheless for all that.

In the triumphant course of his prosperous fate,

He was assassinated by foreign hands.

It was not his son that brought him these blows.

And I lost my son without saving my spouse!

May this frightful example at least be capable of instructing you!

Banish this terror that a priest inspires in you,

Profit from my sins and calm your mind.

OEDIPUS

After the great secret you have taught me,

It is just in my turn that in my gratitude

I make a horrible confidence of my destiny.

When you've learned from this sad conversation

The terrible agreement of your fate and mine

Perhaps, like me, you will shiver with fright.

Destiny made me born to the throne of Corinth.

Still far distant from Corinth and the throne

I look with horror at the chains wherein I was born.

One day, one frightful day, present now in my thoughts,

Cast terror into my frozen soul.

For the first time, by a solemn gift

My young hands were still enriching the altar.

The temple suddenly completely opened.

Terrible traces of blood covered the marbles.

The altar shaken by lengthy tremblings

An invisible hand pushed away my offerings.

And the winds in the midst of bursting lightning

Bore to me this frightening voice:

"Don't come to holy places to soil their purity.

The gods have rejected you from the number of the living.

They won't receive your impious offerings.

Go, take your gifts to the altars of the furies.

Conjure their serpents ready to tear you apart.

Go, these are the gods that you must implore."

While I abandoned my soul to terror

This voice announced to me, would you believe it, madam?

Unheard of felonies to the whole frightened assembly

With which heaven once threatened your son,

Telling me I would be the assassin of my father.

JOCASTA

Ah, gods!

OEDIPUS

That I would be the husband of my mother.

JOCASTA

Where am I? What demon, in uniting our hearts,

Dear prince, has been able to collect so many horrors in us.

OEDIPUS

It's not yet time to shed tears.

You will learn soon enough other subjects for alarms.

Hear me, madam, and you are going to tremble.

I had to exile myself from the breast of my native land.

I feared that my hand, criminal despite myself

To enemy fates would not be faithful,

And suspect to myself, odious to myself,

My virtue dared not struggle against these gods.

I tore myself from the arms of a disconsolate mother.

I left, I ran from country to country.

Everywhere I disguised my birth and my name.

A friend was the sole companion of my steps.

In more than one adventure on this fatal voyage

The god who guided me seconded my courage.

Happy, if I had been able, in one of these battles,

To thwart my destiny by a noble death!

But, no question, I was reserved for parricide.

Finally, I recall that in the fields of Phocida

I don't know through what enchantment

I had forgotten until now this great event.

The hand of the gods, so long suspended over me

Seemed to lift the blindfold that they had placed on my sight.

On a narrow road I found two warriors

On a dazzling chariot pulled by two corsairs;

In this narrow passage, it was necessary to dispute

The vain honor of the frivolous advantage of passing.

I was young and proud and nourished in a rank

Wherein pride always mixed with blood.

Stranger in the breast of a strange land,

I thought myself still on the throne of my father.

And all those that fate offered to my sight

Seemed to me subjects and made to obey me.

I strode toward them and my furious hand

Stopped the impetuous spirit of the corsairs.

These warriors hurled themselves out of the chariot,

Hurried blows rained down on me with fury.

Victory between us was not uncertain.

Powerful gods, I don't know if it was favor or hate

But without doubt for me you were battling against them

And the one and the other finally fell at my feet.

One of the two, I recall, already frozen by age,

Stretched in the dust, observed my face.

He extended his arm to me, he wanted to speak to me.

From his expiring eyes I saw tears spill.

Complete victor that I was, I felt in my soul

Myself as I skewered him— You are shaking, madam.

JOCASTA

Lord, here's Phorbas: they are bringing him here.

OEDIPUS

Alas! My frightful suspicion is going to be clarified!

(Enter Phorbas and others.)

OEDIPUS

Come, wretched old geezer, come, come closer. At his sight

A trouble is reborn in my uneasy soul.

A confused memory again comes to afflict me,

I tremble to see him and to question him.

PHORBAS

Well, is it today that I must perish?

Great queen, have you ordered my death?

You were never unjust except to me.

JOCASTA

Reassure yourself, Phorbas, and reply to the king.

PHORBAS

To the king!

JOCASTA

I am making you appear before him.

PHORBAS

O gods! Laius is dead and you are my master!

You, Lord?

OEDIPUS

Spare us superfluous speech.

You were the only witness to the murder of Laius;

They say you were wounded, trying to defend him.

PHORBAS

Lord, Laius is dead, leave his ashes in peace.

Don't insult, at least, the unhappy fate

Of a faithful subject wounded by your hand.

OEDIPUS

I wounded you? Who, me?

PHORBAS

Satisfy your wish;

Finish by separating me from an importunate life.

Lord, let your arms that the gods deceived

Shed what remains of the blood that escaped you.

And since you recall in this funereal path

Wherein my king—

OEDIPUS

Wretch! Spare me the rest.

I did it all, I see it, that's enough of it. O gods!

At last, after four years you are opening my eyes.

JOCASTA

Alas! Then it's true!

OEDIPUS

What! It was you that my rage

Attacked on the way to Daulis in that narrow passage!

Yes, it's you: vainly, I'm trying to abuse myself.

Everything speaks against me; all serves to accuse me.

And to my astonishment, I cannot fail to recognize you.

PHORBAS

It's true, I saw my master fall under your blows.

You committed the crime and I was suspected.

I lived in chains and you reigned.

OEDIPUS

Go, soon I will do justice on myself in my turn.

Go, leave to me at least the care of my death.

Leave me alone, save me from the sorrowful affront

Of seeing an innocent that I have made wretched.

(Exit Phorbas and the others.)

OEDIPUS

Jocasta, for now jealous fortune

Forbids me forever the tender name of spouse.

You see my felonies; free of your loyalty,

Strike, free me from the horror of being me.

JOCASTA

Alas!

OEDIPUS

Take this sword, instrument of my rage,

Let it serve you today for a more just employment.

Plunge it in my breast.

JOCASTA

What are you doing, Lord?

Stop; moderate this blind sorrow.

Live.

OEDIPUS

What pity interests you for me?

I must die.

JOCASTA

Live, it's I who urge you.

Hear my prayer.

OEDIPUS

I killed your husband.

JOCASTA

But you are my husband.

OEDIPUS

I am through crime.

JOCASTA

It was involuntary.

OEDIPUS

No matter, it was committed.

JOCASTA

O completion of misery.

OEDIPUS

O too funereal marriage! O passion formerly so sweet!

JOCASTA

That's not extinguished; you are my spouse.

OEDIPUS

No, I am no longer so; and my enemy hand

Has not too soon broken the holy bond that links us.

I fill these parts with the misfortune which pursues me.

Beware me, fear the god who is chasing me.

My timid virtue serves only to confuse me,

And I can, henceforth, no longer answer for myself.

Perhaps from the wrath this god shares

The horror of my destiny will reach even you.

Have less pity for so many other victims.

Strike, don't be afraid. You will spare me crimes.

JOCASTA

Don't accuse yourself of such a cruel destiny.

You are unlucky and not criminal.

In that fatal struggle that Daulis saw you render,

You were unaware of the blood your hands were going to shed.

And recalling this frightful memory,

I can only pity myself and not punish you

Live.

OEDIPUS

As for me, how can I live! I must flee you.

Alas! Where will I drag a dying life?

On what wretched shores, in what sad climes,

To shroud the horror that attaches itself to my heels?

Shall I go, still wandering, and fleeing from myself,

To deserve some new diadem by murder?

Shall I go into Corinth where my sad fate

For even greater crimes is still reserved for my hand?

Corinth! never let your detestable shore—

(Enter Dimas.)

DIMAS

Lord, at this moment a stranger is arriving.

He says he's from Corinth and demands to see you.

OEDIPUS

Go, in a moment I am going to receive him.

(to Jocasta)

Farewell: may the source of your tears dissipate.

You will no longer see the inconsolable Oedipus.

It's finished; I've reigned, you no longer have husbands.

By ceasing to be king, I am ceasing to be yours.

I am leaving, I am going to seek in my mortal sorrow

A land where my hand may not be criminal.

And living far from you, without a realm, but as a king,

To justify the tears that you are shedding for me.

CURTAIN

ACT V

OEDIPUS

Finish your regrets and contain your tears.

You pity my exile, for me it has charms.

My flight assures you prompt succor from your misfortunes.

And losing your king you preserve your life.

It is time that I direct the fate of all these people.

I saved this empire by taking the throne.

I will descend from it at least as I mounted it,

My glory will follow me in my adversity.

My fate still renders you life.

I am leaving my children, my throne, my country.

Hear me at least for the last time.

Since you must have a king, consult in my choice.

Philoctetes is powerful, virtuous, intrepid,

His father is a monarch; he was friend of Alcidas,

Let me leave and let him reign. Go find Phorbas.

Let him appear before my eyes, let him not fear me.

My bounties must leave him some mark

And to leave my subjects and my throne like a monarch.

Let them make the foreigner come to my presence.

You, remain.

(Exit Dimas, enter Icarus.)

OEDIPUS

Icarus, is it you that I see?

You, wise guardian of my early years,

You, worthy favorite of my father?

What important subject brings you amongst us?

ICARUS

Lord, Polybius is dead.

OEDIPUS

Ah! What are you telling me?

My father—

ICARUS

You must have expected his death.

Years made him descend to the night of the tomb,

His days were full; he died before my eyes.

OEDIPUS

What's become of you, oracles of our gods?

You who made my too timid virtue tremble,

You who prepared me for the horror of a parricide.

My father is amongst the dead and you deceived me.

Despite you my hands are not soaked in his blood.

Thus, slave to my willful mistake,

Occupied with avoiding an imaginary ill,

I abandoned my life to certain misfortunes

Too credulous artisan of my sad fate!

O heaven! And what then is the excess of my misery,

If the death of my own becomes necessary to me?

If, finding in their ruin an odious happiness,

For me the death of a father is a blessing of the gods?

Let's go, I must leave: I must acquit myself

Of the funeral tribute that his ashes merit.

Let's leave, you be quiet, I see your tears streaming.

Let this silence—

ICARUS

O heaven! Will I dare to speak?

OEDIPUS

Do there still remain misfortunes you have to inform me of?

ICARUS

Will you deign to hear me for a moment without witnesses?

OEDIPUS (to the followers)

Go, withdraw. What's he going to announce to me?

ICARUS

You mustn't think of going to Corinth, Lord.

If you appear there, your death is sworn.

OEDIPUS

Eh! Who would forbid me to enter my realm?

ICARUS:

Another is heir to Polybius' scepter.

OEDIPUS

Is this enough? And this dart, will it be the last?

Pursue, Fate, pursue, you cannot beat me down.

Well! I will go reign: Icarus, let's go battle.

Let's run to present myself to my cowardly subjects.

Among those wretches, prompt to rebel,

At least I can find an honorable death.

Dying amongst the Thebans, I would be culpable.

I must perish as king. Who are my enemies?

Speak, what stranger is seated on my throne?

ICARUS

The son-in-law of Polybius, and Polybius himself,

As he died, placed the crown on his head.

All the people obey their new master.

OEDIPUS

Eh, what! My father too, my father betrayed me?

My father was an accomplice of rebellion?

He kicked me out of the throne!

ICARUS

He did you justice;

You were not his son.

OEDIPUS

Icarus!

ICARUS

Trembling with regret,

I am revealing this terrible secret!

But it is necessary, lord, and the whole province—

OEDIPUS

I am not his son!

ICARUS

No, lord, and this prince

Said it to all as he died. His remorse urged him on.

He renounced you for the blood of our kings.

And as for me, his secret confidant and accomplice,

Fearing the severe justice of the new king,

I came to implore your support in these parts.

OEDIPUS

I wasn't his son! And who am I, great gods?

ICARUS

Heaven that delivered your infancy to my hands

Is covering your birth in profound night;

And I only know that in being born condemned

And on a deserted mountain destined to perish

But for me light would have been ravished from you.

OEDIPUS

In that case my misfortune begins with my life.

From the cradle I was the horror of my house.

Where did I fall into your hands?

ICARUS

On Mount Citheron.

OEDIPUS

Near Thebes?

ICARUS

A Theban who called himself your father

Exposed your infancy in that solitary abode.

Some beneficent god guided my steps toward you.

Pity seized me, I took you in my arms.

I reanimated in you almost extinct warmth.

You were alive, soon I brought you to Corinth.

I presented you to the prince: wonder at your fate!

The prince adopted you in place of his dead son.

And by this adroit maneuver, his happy policy

Affirmed forever his doubtful power.

You were raised under the name of his son,

By this same hand which saved you.

But indeed, the throne was not your place.

Interest put you there, remorse drove you from it.

OEDIPUS

O you who preside over the fortune of kings,

Gods! Must you overwhelm me so many times in one day.

And, preparing your blows with your lying oracles,

Exhaust your miracles against a weak mortal?

But friend, this old geezer from whom you received me,

Have you never seen him since that time?

ICARUS

Never: and perhaps death ravished from you

The only one who could have told from what blood you were born.

But his features have occupied me for a long while.

I was so struck by his image

That I would recognize him if he were to appear.

OEDIPUS

Wretch! Eh! Why seek to know him?

I really ought rather to agree with the gods

To cherish the blindfold which covers my eyes.

I perceive my fate: these cruel researches

Will only disclose new horrors to me.

I know it, but despite the ills I foresee

A curious desire is leading me far from myself.

I cannot remain in this uncertainty.

Suspicion in my misfortune is too harsh a torment.

I abhor the flame with which I intend to enlighten myself.

I fear knowing myself, and cannot bear not knowing myself.

(enter Phorbas)

Ah! Phorbas, come forward!

ICARUS

My shock is intense!

The more I see him, the more— Ah! Lord, it's he himself.

It's him.

PHORBAS (to Icarus)

Pardon me if your unknown features—

ICARUS

What! Don't you remember Mount Citheron any more?

PHORBAS

What?

ICARUS

What! That child that you delivered to my hands,

That child that to death—

PHORBAS

Ah! What are you saying?

And with what recollection are you coming to overwhelm me?

ICARUS

Come, fear not, cease to trouble yourself

You have in these parts nothing but subjects of joy.

Oedipus is that child.

PHORBAS

May heaven's thunder strike you.

Wretch! What have you said?

ICARUS (to Oedipus)

Lord, there's no doubt about it;

Regardless of what this Theban says, he delivered you to my arms.

Your fate is known and therefore your father—

OEDIPUS

O fate which confounds me! O heap of misery!

(to Phorbas)

I was born of you? Heaven would have allowed

That your blood shed—

PHORBAS

You are not my son.

OEDIPUS

Eh, what! Didn't you expose me in my infancy?

PHORBAS

Lord, allow me to flee your presence

And to spare you this horrible conversation.

OEDIPUS

Phorbas, in the name of the gods, don't hide anything from me.

PHORBAS

Leave, lord, flee your childhood and your queen.

OEDIPUS

Just answer me! Resistance is in vain.

That child, destined by you to death—

(pointing to Icarus)

Did you place it in his arms?

PHORBAS

Yes, I gave it to him.

Would that day have been the last of my life!

OEDIPUS

What was his fatherland?

PHORBAS

Thebes was his fatherland.

OEDIPUS

You were not his father?

PHORBAS

Alas! He was born

From a blood more glorious and more unfortunate.

OEDIPUS

Who was he at last?

PHORBAS (casting himself at the king's knees)

Lord, what are you going to do?

OEDIPUS

Get it over with. I intend to know.

PHORBAS

Jocasta was his mother.

ICARUS

And so that's the fruit of my generous efforts?

PHORBAS

What have the two of us done?

OEDIPUS

I didn't expect less.

ICARUS

Lord—

OEDIPUS

Go, cruel ones, leave my presence.

Fear the reward for your frightful benefactions.

Flee! Reserved by you alone for so many horrors,

I will punish you too much for having preserved me.

(Exit Phorbas and Icarus.)

OEDIPUS

Now there's the fulfillment of this execrable oracle,

From which my fear urged the inevitable effect!

At last I see myself by a frightful ending,

Incestuous and parricidal, and yet virtuous.

Miserable virtue, sterile and funereal name,

You by whom I regulated the life I detest,

You were unable to resist my dark rise.

I fell into the snare by trying to avoid it.

A god stronger than you was dragging me toward crime.

Beneath my fugitive feet he hollowed an abyss.

And I was, in my blindness, despite myself,

The slave and tool of an unknown power.

These are all my misdeeds; I don't know of any others.

Pitiless gods, my crimes are yours

And you are punishing me for them? Where am I? What night

Covers with a hideous veil the knowledge that enlightens us?

These walls are stained with blood: I see the Eumenides

Shaking their vengeful torches at parricides.

Thunder, in bursts seems to break over me.

Hell is opening. O Laius, o my father! is it you?

I see, I recognize the mortal wound

That this criminal hand made in your side.

Punish me, avenge yourself on a detested monster,

On a monster that soiled the loins that bore him.

Come closer, drag me into the somber dwellings.

I shall go to my death to frighten ghosts,

Come, I am with you.

(Enter Jocasta, Aegina and the Chorus.)

JOCASTA

Lord, chase away my terror;

Your formidable screams have come even to me.

OEDIPUS

Earth, to swallow me, open your caverns!

JOCASTA

What unforeseen misfortune overwhelms you?

OEDIPUS

My crimes.

JOCASTA

Lord—

OEDIPUS

Flee, Jocasta.

JOCASTA

Ah! Too cruel spouse!

OEDIPUS

Wretched woman! Stop: what name are you uttering?

Me, your spouse! Abandon that abominable title

Which renders us execrable to each other.

JOCASTA

What do I hear?

OEDIPUS

It's over with: our fates are fulfilled.

Laius was my father, and I am your son.

(He leaves.)

FIRST CHARACTER IN THE CHORUS

O Crime!

SECOND CHARACTER IN THE CHORUS

O frightful day! Day terrible forever!

JOCASTA

Aegina, tear me away from this horrible palace.

AEGINA

Alas!

JOCASTA

If so many ills can touch you,

If, without shaking, your hand can still approach me,

Help me, support me, take pity on your queen.

FIRST CHARACTER IN THE CHORUS

Gods! Is this the way your hate ends?

Take back, take back, your funereal blessings,

Cruel ones! It would be better to punish us forever.

(The High Priest enters.)

HIGH PRIEST

Folks, a happy calm is warding off the storms

A most serene sun is rising above your heads.

Contagious fires are no longer lit.

Your tombs which were opening are already shut.

Death is fleeing and the god of heaven and earth

Is announcing his blessings through the voice of thunder.

(The rumble of thunder is heard and bursts of lightning seen.)

JOCASTA

What outbursts! Where am I? What am I hearing?

Barbarians!

HIGH PRIEST

It's over with, and the gods are satisfied.

Laius, from the breast of the dead, is ceasing to pursue you.

He permits you to reign and still love.

The blood of Oedipus has finally sufficed his wrath.

CHORUS

God!

JOCASTA

O my son! Alas! Shall I say my spouse?

O most terrifying assembly of most dear names.

He is dead then?

HIGH PRIEST

He is living and the fate which overwhelms him

Seems to separate him from the living and the dead.

He has deprived himself of the light before expiring.

I saw him thrust this sword that had soaked

In his father's blood into his eyes.

He has fulfilled his fate; and this fatal moment

Ought to be the first sign of the safety of Thebans.

Such is the order of heaven whose furor is relaxing

As it pleases, it gives justice or mercy to mortals.

Its arrows are exhausted on this unfortunate son.

Live, it pardons you.

JOCASTA (beating herself)

And as for me, I am punishing myself.

Reserved by a terrible power for incest

Death is the sole blessing, the sole god that remains to

me.

Laius, receive my blood, I am with you amongst the dead.

I lived virtuously and I am dying without remorse.

CHORUS

O unfortunate queen! O fate that I abhor!

JOCASTA

Just pity my son, since he is still breathing.

Priests, and you, Thebans who are my subjects,

Honor my funeral pyre, and think forever

That amidst the horrors destiny oppressed me with

I made the gods who forced crime on me to blush.

CURTAIN

ABOUT THE AUTHOR

Frank J. Morlock has written and translated many plays since retiring from the legal profession in 1992. His translations have also appeared on Project Gutenberg, the Alexandre Dumas Père web page, Literature in the Age of Napoléon, Infinite Artistries.com, and Munsey's (formerly Blackmask). In 2006 he received an award from the North American Jules Verne Society for his translations of Verne's plays. He lives and works in México.

www.ingramcontent.com/pod-product-compliance
Lightning Source LLC
LaVergne TN
LVHW041627070426
835507LV00008B/490